LET'S FIND OUT ABOUT

Christian Churches

Sarah Medina

www.raintreepublishers.co.uk
Visit our website to find out more information about Raintree books.

To order:
 Phone 44 (0) 1865 888112
 Send a fax to 44 (0) 1865 314091
Visit the Raintree Bookshop at www.raintreepublishers.co.uk to browse our catalogue and order online.

First published in Great Britain by Raintree, Halley Court, Jordan Hill, Oxford, OX2 8EJ, part of Harcourt Education.
Raintree is a registered trademark of Harcourt Education Ltd.

© Harcourt Education Ltd 2006.
First published in paperback in 2007.
The moral right of the proprietor has been asserted.

Editorial: Daniel Nunn and Sarah Chappelow
Design: Ron Kamen and Philippa Baile
Picture research: Hannah Taylor and Sally Claxton
Production: Duncan Gilbert
Religious consultant: Jo Turkas, Assistant Schools Officer, Canterbury Cathedral

Originated by Modern Age
Printed and bound in China by WKT

ISBN 10: 1 844 21138 X (hardback)
ISBN 13: 978 1 844 21138 8 (hardback)
10 09 08 07 06
10 9 8 7 6 5 4 3 2 1

ISBN 10: 1 844 21145 2 (paperback)
ISBN 13: 978 1 844 21145 6 (paperback)
11 10 09 08 07 06
10 9 8 7 6 5 4 3 2 1

British Library Cataloguing in Publication Data
Medina, Sarah
   Let's find out about Christian churches
   1. Church buildings – Juvenile literature
   2. Christianity – Customs and practices – Juvenile literature
   I. Title II. Christian churches
   260
A full catalogue record for this book is available from the British Library.

Acknowledgements
The publishers would like to thank the following for permission to reproduce photographs:

Alamy Images pp. **5** (Linda Reinink-Smith), **10** (F 1 Online), **12 top left** (Bildarchiv Monheim GmbH), **12 top right** (World Religions Photo Library), **13** (Bildarchiv Monheim GmbH); Art Directors p. **4**; Circa Photo Library pp. **16, 18**; Corbis pp. **14 top** (David Reed), **21** (Hulton-Deutsch Collection), **22** (Joseph Sohm); Getty Images/Photodisc pp. **14 bottom, 15 top**; PA Photos p. **25**; Trip pp. **6** (Tony Freeman), **7** (David Butcher), **8** (C. Treppe), **9** (Bob Turner), **11** (Constance Toms), **12 bottom** (H. Rogers), **15 bottom** (H. Rogers), **17** (K. Cardwell), **19** (H. Rogers), **20** (S. Grant), **23** (H. Rogers), **24** (H. Rogers), **26** (S. Grant), **27** (Jeff Greenberg).

Cover photograph of a church in a snowy field reproduced with permission of Corbis Royalty Free.

Every effort has been made to contact copyright holders of any material reproduced in this book. Any omissions will be rectified in subsequent printings if notice is given to the publishers.

The paper used to print this book comes from sustainable resources.

Contents

Words appearing in the text in bold, **like this**, are explained in the Glossary. The Christian words used in this book are listed with a pronunciation guide on page 29.

What is a church?

A church (with a small "c") is a special building where Christians meet and **worship**. Worship is a way for people to show their love and respect for God. Christians worship by praying, singing, and learning about the **Bible**.

Christians are people who follow the religion of **Christianity**. Christianity is one of the main religions in the world. This means that churches are found in many different countries. In fact, churches can be found everywhere – from the biggest cities to the smallest villages!

This church in the United Kingdom is very old. New parts have been added to it over hundreds of years.

The word *church* comes from an old Greek word that means "house of God". This means that for Christians a church is a place where God is. Because of this, millions of Christians go to church every week to spend time with God.

Did you know

The oldest church in the world is believed to be in Syria. It is called the Kaneesat Um Zunnar church. There have been churches in Syria for nearly 2,000 years.

This church in Alaska, in the United States, looks out over the sea.

Christians and Christianity

Christianity began just over 2,000 years ago in a part of the Middle East called Palestine (now also called Israel). During this time, many people started to believe that a man called **Jesus** was not an ordinary man. They believed that Jesus was God's son, and that God had sent Jesus to save them. These people were the first Christians.

The leaders in Palestine were worried that Jesus was so popular. They killed Jesus on a wooden **cross**. Christians believe that Jesus came back to life and that he lives with God in heaven.

Christians believe that they can talk to God and Jesus by praying.

After Jesus died, some of his followers travelled to different countries to tell other people about him. Today, there are hundreds of millions of Christians in the world.

Did you know

Christians use the word *Church* (with a capital "C") to mean a group of Christian people. Not all Christians belong to the same Church. There are three main Churches. These are the **Protestant** Church, the **Roman Catholic** Church, and the **Orthodox** Church.

Christians from countries all over the world love to worship together.

Churches big and small

Christian churches come in all shapes and sizes! Some are big enough to hold hundreds of people. Others are small rooms in houses. Most are somewhere in-between. Churches can also look very different from each other. Some look very old. Others are new and modern.

Some people worship outside, under the sun!

Cathedrals are really important churches for Christians. They are often very old and large, and have beautiful decorations. Most cathedrals are built in the middle of big cities. They are usually the biggest churches for miles around.

It can take a long time to build a cathedral. In Barcelona, Spain, there is a cathedral called the Sagrada Familia. People started to build it in 1882. It will not be finished until 2041 – more than 150 years later!

St Peter's Cathedral in Rome, Italy, is the most important cathedral for Roman Catholics.

Church buildings

Church buildings can hold lots of clues about when they were built and what happened there. The first Christian churches were built in the shape of a rectangle, with a wooden ceiling. Inside there was one large **aisle** down the middle and two smaller aisles at the sides. These were separated by tall **columns**.

Hundreds of years later, churches were built in the shape of a **cross** to remind people how **Jesus** died. The ceilings were made of stone, so the walls had to be very thick. This meant that the windows were very small. These churches were often quite dark inside.

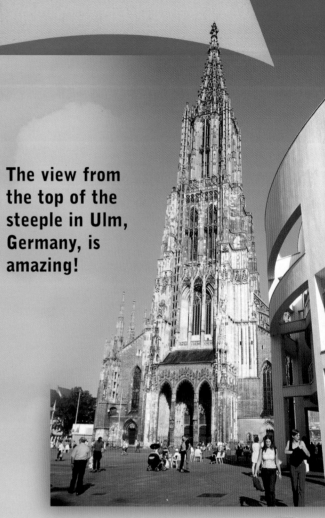

The view from the top of the steeple in Ulm, Germany, is amazing!

Did you know

The tallest **steeple** in the world is in Ulm, Germany. It is 160 metres (175 yards) tall. That is as tall as 100 people standing on each others' shoulders!

The Crystal Cathedral in California, in the United States, is built almost entirely of glass and steel.

As people learned how to make better buildings, churches became larger and brighter. They often had huge **stained-glass windows**. Modern churches have many different styles. Some are even round, so that everyone can see each other!

Inside a church

Even though church buildings can look very different, most churches have some things that are the same.

The altar is a special table that is used during **worship**. It is usually found at the front of the church.

an altar

The pulpit is a place where a church leader can stand and talk to people. It is high up so that everyone can hear and see.

a pulpit

You can see the altar, font, and nave in this church.

altar

font

nave

This diagram shows the layout of the inside of a typical church.

The nave is the area where most people sit. In older churches, people sit on wooden benches called pews. Newer churches have normal chairs.

In many Churches, water is used in a special **service** to welcome new Christians. This is called **baptism**. The water is held in a bowl called a font, inside a decorated wood or stone stand.

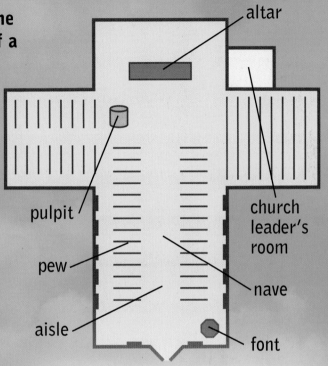

altar

pulpit

pew

aisle

church leader's room

nave

font

a font

> *A Christian view*
> At my baby sister's baptism, Mum, Dad, and some friends stood by the church font. They all said some special words, and then the minister put some water on Chloe's head. She stayed asleep the whole time.
> *Tommy, age ten, from the United Kingdom*

A beautiful place

Christian churches are often very beautiful places. People like to **worship** God in the best possible surroundings.

Churches are decorated in many different ways. Some have carved walls and ceilings, or bright banners and paintings. Others have lovely **stained-glass windows**. Some stained-glass windows tell stories from the **Bible**. They also make a church brighter. They look especially pretty when the sun shines through them.

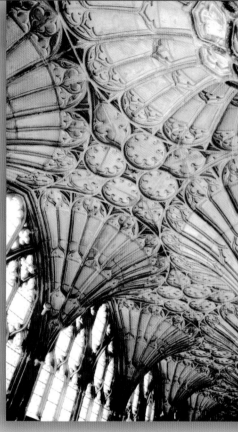

If you look up in a church, you may be surprised to see an amazing ceiling!

Stained-glass windows told Christian stories in pictures in the days when many people could not read.

In some Churches, saints are an important part of worship. Saints are people who some Christians believe were very close to God. Pictures of the saints, called icons, often decorate **Orthodox** churches. **Roman Catholic** churches may have statues of saints in them.

This icon from a church in Italy shows the baby Jesus with his mother Mary.

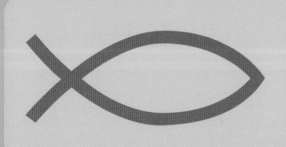

Did you know

One important symbol for Christians is a picture of a fish. Many of the first Christians were fishermen.

church workers

Lots of different people work in Christian churches. Some of them are paid for their work. Many others work as **volunteers**.

Every church has a leader. This person is sometimes called the **minister**. During a church **service**, the minister reads from the **Bible**, prays, and gives a talk called a **sermon**. Ministers also lead special services, such as **baptisms** and weddings.

Sometimes, other people help the minister to lead the service. People help in other ways too. They keep the church clean or decorate it with flowers. Even young people can help in a church. They can take care of small children, or help to make tea and coffee.

This church minister is leading a Sunday service.

In most churches, Christians love to make music. During **worship**, Christians sing special songs, called hymns. Some churches have music groups that lead the singing. They play instruments such as guitars, recorders, and tambourines. Many churches have an organ too.

Music is an important way for Christians to worship God.

Worship in a church

Christians go to church to **worship** God. One way of doing this is to read the **Bible**. Christians believe that, in the Bible, God tells them the best way to live their lives.

A Christian view

I go to church with my family every Sunday. We all sing and pray together, and then I go to **Sunday School** with the other children.
Claudia, age seven, from Connecticut, USA

Christian children learn about the Bible in Sunday School.

Most church **services** include a **sermon**. This is a talk given by the church **minister** or another leader. The sermon is usually based on Bible teachings.

Christians also go to church to pray. They believe that prayer is a way of talking to God. Some prayers said in church, such as the **Lord's Prayer**, have been written down. Other prayers are just like talking to someone you know.

Celebrating **Communion** is an important way for Christians to remember **Jesus**. They share a little wine and bread, and say special prayers.

In Communion, Christians remember the last meal that Jesus had with his followers.

Special Occasions

Churches are places where Christians can celebrate special days together. A wedding is a **service** in which two people who love each other get married. It is a very happy occasion!

When someone dies, the person's family and friends remember him or her in a church service called a funeral. They often sing and say prayers, and talk about their loved one.

The most important festival is Easter. On Good Friday, Christians think about how **Jesus** died. On Easter Sunday, they celebrate their belief that Jesus came back to life and that he lives with God in heaven.

Many Christians get married in church.

Did you know
Christians in **Protestant** and **Roman Catholic** Churches celebrate Christmas on 25 December, but **Orthodox** Christians celebrate it on 6 or 7 January.

At Christmas time, Christians celebrate when Jesus was born. They may decorate their church with candles, a Christmas tree, and a **Nativity scene**. This shows the Christmas story.

These Christians are celebrating Christmas in Bethlehem, where Jesus was born.

A place to meet

A lot more goes on in a church than just **worship** on Sundays. Churches are a great place for people to meet and spend time with each other.

Some churches have baby and toddler groups, where parents can talk to each other while their children play. These may be held in church halls, which have plenty of space for children to play.

These people are enjoying a Christmas meal together at a church in the United States.

Many activity groups for children, such as Scouts and Guides, hold their meetings in church buildings.

As children get older, they can go to church clubs in the school holidays. Here, they can learn about **Christianity** and do fun activities, such as arts and crafts or sports. Sometimes, churches run youth clubs for older children too. There may also be classes they can go to, where they can learn more about being a Christian.

The Church is a kind of Christian "family". People in church try to care for each other. Sometimes, Christians visit people who are ill or sad. They help them by talking and praying with them. They can also help them with chores.

Spending time in a church

Children are an important part of church life!

Churches are special places for Christians, where they **worship** God by praying, singing, and learning about the **Bible**. Churches often feel very peaceful. People do not usually run or shout in church. They are careful about how they act.

In the past, many Christians used to wear their best clothes to church. They called these nice clothes their "Sunday best"! Dressing nicely was one way they showed respect.

Ministers used to wear special long robes during church services. Today, they sometimes wear "normal" clothes, just like other people!

Today, some churches and church **services** can be quite **formal**, but many churches are very relaxed. Some people dress carefully for church, but this is not so important any more. The most important thing for Christians is that they go to church ready to love and worship God.

"

A Christian view

When I go to church, I see my friends. We listen to stories about **Jesus**. Sometimes, we get to join in. It's fun!
Jake, age eight, from Melbourne, Australia

"

Worship at home

Christians do not just **worship** God at church. They also worship God in their own homes.

Christians like to say thank you to God. They do this by singing and praying. At mealtimes, Christians sometimes say a special prayer to thank God for their food. They call this "saying **grace**". Christians often say prayers before they go to sleep too.

When Christians say grace, they are thanking God for providing food for them to eat.

House groups are a popular way for Christians to meet up.

Some Christians read the **Bible** at home every day. Christian families make time every day to pray and talk together. They talk about what it is like to be a Christian. They often help each other out, and they ask for God's help too.

In some Churches, Christians meet in other people's homes to worship God. These meetings are sometimes called Bible study groups. People read and talk about the Bible together. They usually pray, and sometimes they sing too.

Christianity around the world

The Christian religion began just over 2,000 years ago. Since the earliest days of **Christianity**, Christians have travelled all over the world. Today, Christians live in nearly every country. The United States, Brazil, and Mexico are the countries with the largest numbers of Christians.

Today, Christianity is the world's largest religion. There are hundreds of millions of Christians worldwide. In fact, out of every three people in the world, one person is a Christian.

Numbers of Christians around the world (numbers are not exact)

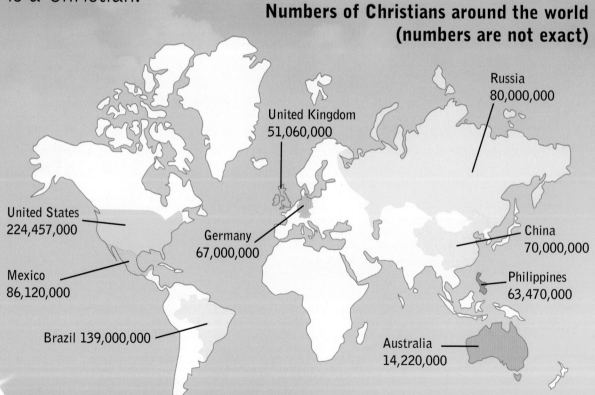

Russia
80,000,000

United Kingdom
51,060,000

United States
224,457,000

Germany
67,000,000

China
70,000,000

Mexico
86,120,000

Philippines
63,470,000

Brazil 139,000,000

Australia
14,220,000

Christian words

These are Christian words that have been used in this book. You can find out how to say them by reading the pronunciation guide in the brackets after each word.

aisle [eye-ul] – long, narrow space between rows of seats in a church

altar [ol-tur] – special table used during worship in a church

baptism [bap-tis-um] – service that celebrates when someone joins the Christian church

Bible [bi-bul] – holy book for Christians

cathedral [cath-ee-drul] – very large and important church

Christianity [cris-tee-an-i-tee] – religion that follows the teachings of Jesus and the Bible

Communion [cum-yoo-nee-un] – special service in which Christians share bread and wine to remember Jesus

font [font] – special bowl of water used in a baptism service

hymn [him] – a religious song, usually sung in church

icon [eye-con] – statue or painting that shows Jesus or a saint

nave [nayv] – area of a church where most people sit

pew [pyoo] – wooden bench that people sit on in church

pulpit [pul-pit] – stand from which the priest or minister can lead the service

saint [saynt] – person who Christians believe was especially close to God

sermon [sur-mun] – special kind of lesson in a church, when the minister talks about Christianity

Glossary

aisle long, narrow space between rows of seats in a church

baptism special service when someone joins the Christian church

Bible holy book for Christians

Christianity religion that follows the teachings of Jesus

columns tall poles that hold up a building

Communion special service in which Christians share bread and wine to remember Jesus

cross a post with another piece of wood across it. Jesus died on a large cross made of wood.

formal serious

grace special prayer said before mealtimes

Jesus Christians believe that Jesus is God's son

Lord's Prayer popular Christian prayer that Jesus used

minister leader in a Christian church

Nativity scene model scene showing the story of the birth of Jesus

Orthodox type of Christianity, found mainly in countries such as Russia, Greece, and Ethiopia

Protestant type of Christianity

Roman Catholic type of Christianity. The Pope is the leader of the Roman Catholic Church.

sermon special kind of lesson in a church, when the minister talks about Christianity

service time when Christians worship God in church

stained-glass window beautiful window made using coloured glass

steeple the spire on top of a church tower

Sunday School classes for children who go to church

volunteer person who works without being paid

worship spending special time with God. Christians worship God by praying, singing, and reading the Bible.

Finding out more

Visiting a church

Christians welcome visitors to their churches. In fact, many people who do not usually go to church enjoy spending time in churches. They may be interested in finding out about the church's history. They may love the beautiful buildings, the stained-glass windows, and other art. They may simply feel that the church is a special place where they can sit quietly and think.

When people visit a church, they should always behave respectfully. It is important to remember that a church is a place of God for Christians. Normally, people do not make too much noise or rush around. If they see someone praying, it is especially important not to be noisy. People are allowed to walk around and touch most parts of a church but some areas, such as the altar, may be out of bounds.

More books to read

Celebrations: Christmas, Mandy Ross (Heinemann Library, 2001)

Celebrations: Easter, Anita Ganeri (Heinemann Library, 2001)

Holy Places: The Vatican, Vicky Parker (Heinemann Library, 2002)

Religions of the World: Christianity, Sue Penney (Heinemann Library, 2002)

Useful websites

www.educhurch.org.uk/pupils/index.html
This website compares three churches. It looks at people who worship there, and what you can see and do inside and outside the churches.

www.request.org.uk/infants/infants.htm
This website looks at what it means to be a Christian – from the things that Christians do to what church buildings are like.

Disclaimer
All the Internet addresses (URLs) given in this book were valid at the time of going to press. However, due to the dynamic nature of the Internet, some addresses may have changed, or sites may have ceased to exist since publication. While the author and publishers regret any inconvenience this may cause readers, no responsibility for any such changes can be accepted by either the author or the publishers.

Index